A CENTURY OF
CARDIFF

Wood Street, Cardiff, in the 1920s. (*Western Mail and Echo*)

A CENTURY OF
CARDIFF

JOHN O'SULLIVAN

First published in 2000 by Sutton Publishing Limited

This new paperback edition first published in 2007 by Sutton Publishing

Reprinted in 2013 by
The History Press
The Mill, Brimscombe Port,
Stroud, Gloucestershire, GL5 2QG
www.thehistorypress.co.uk

Copyright © John O'Sullivan, 2000, 2013
Copyright © 'Britain: A Century of Change', Roger Hudson, 2000, 2013

All rights reserved. No part of this publication may be reproduced, stored in a retrieval system, or transmitted, in any form or by any means, electronic, mechanical, photocopying, recording or otherwise, without the prior permission of the publisher and copyright holder.

The author has asserted the moral right to be identified as the author of this work.

British Library Cataloguing in Publication Data
A catalogue record for this book is available from the British Library.

ISBN 978-0-7509-4922-4

Front endpaper: Cardiff Docks, 1923. (*Cardiff Maritime Museum*)
Back endpaper: Cardiff Bay, with the new barrage, completed in 1999 to create a marina at The Bay which will be the focus of events in Cardiff in the new millennium. (*County Hall Archives*)
Half title page: The figurehead of Captain Scott's ship, the *Terra Nova*. (*Cardiff Maritime Museum*)
Title page: Cardiff Arms Park in the 1930s. (*collection of Arthur Weston Evans*)

This book is dedicated to
my late wife Eileen

Typeset in Photina.
Typesetting and origination by
Sutton Publishing.
Printed and bound in England.

Cardiff-born Billy Boston, one of the greatest twentieth-century rugby league players in the world. (*Author's collection*)

Contents

BRITAIN: A CENTURY OF CHANGE *Roger Hudson*	7
CARDIFF: AN INTRODUCTION	13
THE AGE OF DISCOVERY	19
WAR AND PEACE	27
BETWEEN THE WARS	33
UNDER ATTACK	43
WELCOME TO EMPIRE	57
THE MEMORABLE '60S	65
THE ROAD TO FAME	77
JIM'S DEN – NO. 10	83
THE 1980S AND A PAPAL VISIT	87
THE 1990S	95
ACKNOWLEDGEMENTS	121

The Lord Mayor, Alderman Gerard Turnbull, with all the members of the former City Council after its last meeting following local government reorganisation in 1974.

Britain: A Century of Change

Churchill in RAF uniform giving his famous victory sign, 1948.
(Illustrated London News)

A CENTURY of CARDIFF

The sixty years ending in 1900 were a period of huge transformation for Britain. Railway stations, post-and-telegraph offices, police and fire stations, gasworks and gasometers, new livestock markets and covered markets, schools, churches, football grounds, hospitals and asylums, water pumping stations and sewerage plants totally altered the urban scene, and the country's population tripled with more than seven out of ten people being born in or moving to the towns. The century that followed, leading up to the Millennium's end in 2000, was to be a period of even greater change.

When Queen Victoria died in 1901, she was measured for her coffin by her grandson Kaiser Wilhelm, the London prostitutes put on black mourning and the blinds came down in the villas and terraces spreading out from the old town centres. These centres were reachable by train and tram, by the new bicycles and still newer motor cars, were connected by the new telephone, and lit by gas or even electricity. The shops may have been full of British-made cotton and woollen clothing but the grocers and butchers were selling cheap Danish bacon, Argentinian beef, Australasian mutton and tinned or dried fish and fruit from Canada, California and South Africa. Most of these goods were carried in British-built-and-crewed ships burning Welsh steam coal.

Crowds celebrate Armistice Day outside Buckingham Palace as the royal family appears on the balcony, 1918. *(Illustrated London News)*

As the first decade moved on, the Open Spaces Act meant more parks, bowling greens and cricket pitches. The First World War transformed the place of women, as they took over many men's jobs. Its other legacies were the war memorials which joined the statues of Victorian worthies in main squares round the land. After 1918 death duties and higher taxation bit hard, and a quarter of England changed hands in the space of only a few years.

The multiple shop – the chain store – appeared in the high street: Marks & Spencer, Sainsburys, Maypole, Lipton's, Home & Colonial, the Fifty Shilling Tailor, Burton, Boots, W.H. Smith. The shopper was spoilt for choice, attracted by the brash fascias and advertising hoardings for national brands like Bovril, Pears Soap, and Ovaltine. Many new buildings began to be seen, such as garages, motor showrooms, picture palaces (cinemas), 'palais de dance', and ribbons of 'semis' stretched along the roads and new bypasses and onto the new estates nudging the green belts.

During the 1920s cars became more reliable and sophisticated as well as commonplace, with developments like the electric self-starter making them easier for women to drive. Who wanted to turn a crank handle in the new short skirt? This was, indeed, the electric age as much as the motor era. Trolley buses, electric trams and trains extended mass transport and electric light replaced gas in the street and the home, which itself was groomed by the vacuum cleaner.

A major jolt to the march onward and upward was administered by the Great Depression of the early 1930s. The older British industries – textiles, shipbuilding, iron, steel, coal – were already under pressure from foreign competition when this worldwide slump arrived. Luckily there were new diversions to alleviate the misery. The 'talkies' arrived in the cinemas; more and more radios and gramophones were to be found in people's homes; there were new women's magazines, with fashion, cookery tips and problem pages; football pools; the flying feats of women pilots like Amy Johnson; the Loch Ness Monster; cheap chocolate and the drama of Edward VIII's abdication.

Houghton of Aston Villa beats goalkeeper Crawford of Blackburn to score the second of four goals, 1930s. *(Illustrated London News)*

Things were looking up again by 1936 and new light industry was booming in the Home Counties as factories struggled to keep up with the demand for radios, radiograms, cars and electronic goods, including the first television sets. The threat from Hitler's Germany meant rearmament, particularly of the airforce, which stimulated aircraft and aero engine firms. If you were lucky and lived in the south, there was good money to be earned. A semi-detached house cost £450, a Morris Cowley £150. People may have smoked like chimneys but life expectancy, since 1918, was up by 15 years while the birth rate had almost halved.

In some ways it is the little memories that seem to linger longest from the Second World War: the kerbs painted white to show up in the blackout, the rattle of ack-ack shrapnel on roof tiles, sparrows killed by bomb blast. The biggest damage, apart from London, was in the south-west (Plymouth, Bristol) and the Midlands (Coventry, Birmingham). Postwar reconstruction was rooted in the Beveridge Report which set out the expectations for the Welfare State. This, together with the nationalisation of the Bank of England, coal, gas, electricity and the railways, formed the programme of the Labour government in 1945.

Times were hard in the late 1940s, with rationing even more stringent than during the war. Yet this was, as has been said, 'an innocent and well-behaved era'. The first let-up came in 1951 with the Festival of Britain and there was another fillip in 1953 from the Coronation, which incidentally gave a huge boost to the spread of TV. By 1954 leisure motoring had been resumed but the Comet – Britain's best hope for taking on the American aviation industry – suffered a series of mysterious crashes. The Suez debacle of 1956 was followed by an acceleration in the withdrawal from Empire, which had begun in 1947 with the Independence of India. Consumerism was truly born with the advent of commercial TV and most homes soon boasted washing machines, fridges, electric irons and fires.

WAAF personnel tracing the movement of flying bombs and Allied fighters on a plotting table, 1944. *(Illustrated London News)*

The *Lady Chatterley* obscenity trial in 1960 was something of a straw in the wind for what was to follow in that decade. A collective loss of inhibition seemed to sweep the land, as the Beatles and the Rolling Stones transformed popular music, and retailing, cinema and the theatre were revolutionised. Designers, hairdressers, photo-graphers and models moved into places vacated by an Establishment put to flight by the new breed of satirists spawned by *Beyond the Fringe* and *Private Eye*.

In the 1970s Britain seems to have suffered a prolonged hangover after the excesses of the previous decade. Ulster, inflation and union troubles were not made up for by entry into the EEC, North Sea Oil, Women's Lib or, indeed, Punk Rock. Mrs Thatcher applied the corrective in the 1980s, as the country moved over more and more from its old manufacturing base to providing services, consulting, advertising, and expertise in the 'invisible' market of high finance or in IT.

The post-1945 townscape has seen changes to match those in the worlds of work, entertainment and politics. In 1952 the Clean Air Act served notice on smogs and pea-souper fogs, smuts and blackened buildings, forcing people to stop burning coal and go over to smokeless sources of heat and energy. In the same decade some of the best urban building took place in the 'new towns' like Basildon, Crawley, Stevenage and Harlow. Elsewhere open warfare was declared on slums and what was labelled inadequate, cramped, back-to-back, two-up, two-down, housing. The new 'machine for living in' was a flat in a high-rise block. The architects and planners who promoted these were in league with the traffic engineers, determined to keep the motor car moving whatever the price in multi-storey car parks, meters, traffic wardens and ring roads. The old pollutant, coal smoke, was replaced by petrol and diesel exhaust, and traffic noise.

Fast food was no longer only a pork pie in a pub or fish-and-chips. There were Indian curry houses, Chinese take-aways and American-style hamburgers, while the drinker could get away from beer in a wine bar. Under the impact of television the big Gaumonts and Odeons closed or were rebuilt as multi-screen cinemas, while the palais de dance gave way to discos and clubs.

From the late 1960s the introduction of listed buildings and conservation areas, together with the growth of preservation societies, put a brake on 'comprehensive redevelopment'. The end of the century and the start of the Third Millennium saw new challenges to the health of towns and the wellbeing of the nine out of ten people who now live urban lives. The fight is on to prevent town centres from dying, as patterns of housing and shopping change, and edge-of-town supermarkets exercise the attractions of one-stop shopping. But as banks and department stores close, following the haberdashers, greengrocers, butchers and ironmongers, there are signs of new growth such as farmers' markets, and corner stores acting as pick-up points where customers collect shopping ordered on-line from web sites.

Futurologists tell us that we are in stage two of the consumer revolution: a shift from mass consumption to mass customisation driven by a desire to have things that fit us and our particular lifestyle exactly, and for better service. This must offer hope for small city-centre shop premises, as must the continued attraction of physical shopping, browsing and being part of a crowd: in a word, 'shoppertainment'. Another hopeful trend for towns is the growth in the number of young

A CENTURY of CARDIFF

Manchester during the Commonwealth Games in 2002. The city, like others all over the country, has experienced massive redevelopment and rejuvenation in recent years. *(Chris Makepeace)*

people postponing marriage and looking to live independently, alone, where there is a buzz, in 'swinging single cities'. Theirs is a 'flats-and-cafés' lifestyle, in contrast to the 'family suburbs', and certainly fits in with government's aim of building 60 per cent of the huge amount of new housing needed on 'brown' sites, recycled urban land. There looks to be plenty of life in the British town yet.

Cardiff: An Introduction

Cardiff became the greatest coal-exporting port in the world in 1913 yet, just over 100 years earlier, it had been little more than a village, with a Norman castle (still to be rebuilt by the 3rd Marquess of Bute) and a postal address near Llantrisant, an ancient town twelve miles to the north.

The money of the Butes, the richest family in the world, and the suffering of the starving, ragged Irish who sought refuge from the Great Famine of the 1840s were the contrasting foundation stones of the town, which grew into a city in 1905 and was acclaimed the capital of Wales in 1955.

The Irish, who lived in seventy-three ghettos in Cardiff towards the end of the nineteenth century, built the docks, steelworks and railways with money invested by the 2nd Marquess of Bute. He came to Cardiff from the ancestral home of Mountstuart, on the Isle of Bute, and obtained the mineral rights for most of the South Wales valleys. Like a magnet, he attracted other wealthy men to Cardiff.

The docks brought in seamen from all corners of the world, making Cardiff a great cosmopolitan area with people of many races and religions living side by side in an area which became known as Tiger Bay. The Bay was a cauldron of tension as Arabs and Africans, West Indians and Spanish, Chinese and Maltese, Greeks and Italians, Scandinavians and English, Irish and Welsh, rivalled each other for jobs on sea and shore.

The native Welsh, who had resented the influx of Irish refugees in the mid-1800s, were helpless against the tide of newcomers. Each wave staked its claim to a small part of the prosperity of the bustling port on the Bristol Channel, which boasted the second highest tides in the world.

Inevitably there was trouble with street fights between the different groups that struggled for survival in the slums and ghettos while millionaires traded on the Cardiff Stock Exchange, where the world's first £1 million pound deal was struck. The Exchange was only a few yards from where extreme poverty was the hallmark of the streets of Tiger Bay. Policemen dared not walk alone there, where prostitution and street corner gambling, drinking and brawling, were prominent pastimes.

A CENTURY of CARDIFF

Cardiff was where Captain Scott's ship, the *Terra Nova*, came to load up with provisions. These were donated by the cream of Cardiff society, who toasted the great explorer at a dinner at the Royal Hotel. The ship sailed from Cardiff on the first leg of its ill-fated voyage to Antarctica.

Life in Tiger Bay and the Irish ghettos was in stark contrast to what was happening in the once green fields of Cathays. There, at the beginning of the twentieth century, what has often been described as the finest civic centre in Europe was taking shape.

A town hall, law courts and museum, made of brilliant white Portland stone, were new landmarks at the front of a complex on which the university colleges of Cardiff, the Temple of Peace, the Welsh Office, the Glamorgan county hall and the police headquarters were to be built at various times. It was no surprise when Cardiff was elevated to the rank of city in 1905, although it had to wait another fifty years before it was named as the capital of Wales.

In 1912 the New Theatre, still flourishing at the end of the century, was opened on the corner of Greyfriars and Park Place. Through the following decades the city's role as a centre of culture and entertainment developed dramatically with the building of the Prince of Wales Theatre (now a public house), the Sherman Theatre, St David's Hall, the Cardiff International Arena and Chapter Arts Centre. The city was chosen as the base of the Welsh National Opera Company and companies like Hijinx, Everyman and Orbit. The Welsh College of Music and Drama was established in the castle grounds in 1949. A number of its famous students are featured in this book.

Cardiff is also one of the greatest media centres of Britain, with BBC Wales TV and Radio, HTV, the Welsh Language Channel S4C, Red Dragon Radio and independent production companies active within its boundaries.

The history of Cardiff in the twentieth century has been recorded in the pages of the *Western Mail*, *South Wales Evening Express*, *South Wales Echo* and *Cardiff Times*. Journalists from the newspapers have made a big impact in Britain and the world, and some of these too are included in this book.

It was a notice in the window of the *Western Mail* building at the Monument end of St Mary Street that revealed to thousands in the streets outside that Mafeking had been relieved in 1900. It was the *Western Mail* siren which told the people of Cardiff that the First World

The 3rd Marquess of Bute who died in 1900, at the end of a century in which he and his father before him did so much to make Cardiff the greatest coal-exporting port in the world.
(*Cardiff Castle Archives*)

AN INTRODUCTION

War had ended at 11 a.m. on 11 November 1918. Hundreds of Cardiff men had been killed in the war including members of 'The Pals', recruited at the outbreak of war in 1914.

Orchestral concerts, especially at the Park Hall under the leadership of Garforth Mortimor, and society balls were features of the 1920s – a decade in which wounded victims of the war begged openly on the streets. The General Strike of 1926 brought hardship to the whole of Britain and soup kitchens were set up in Cardiff as well as in the mining towns of South Wales. But the gloom was lifted in 1927 when Cardiff City won the FA Cup by beating Arsenal 1–0 at Wembley. King George VI called for an encore of the singing of 'Abide With Me'.

The economic problem got worse in the hungry '30s. Jobless miners sang in the streets of Cardiff and London for pennies and out-of-work seamen gathered at Penniless Point, on the corner of James Street and Bute Street, to beg a handout from the fortunate few signing off the ships – a scene vividly captured by artist Jack Sullivan, some of whose fine work is included in the book.

Racial tension grew as whites fought blacks and blacks fought blacks for the few jobs that were available. When the Spanish Civil War broke out, Blackshirts marched in Grangetown in support of Britain's fascist leader Oswald Mosley and the Spanish dictator Franco. Left-wing groups clashed with the Blackshirts, who failed in a bid to hijack a ship at Cardiff Docks to join Franco in Spain, following the mass murder of hundreds of student priests. Had they succeeded they would have been fighting not only the Spanish Communists but also the people of Cardiff and South Wales who were fighting against Franco.

The Princess of Wales at a rugby international at the National Ground. (*Western Mail and Echo*)

The Spanish Civil War was only the prelude to the Second World War, in which Cardiff was in the front line. The first German bombs fell on the city in July 1940 but the biggest raids were on 2 and 3 January 1941, when large areas of Grangetown and Riverside were destroyed by German parachute mines, high explosive bombs and incendiaries.

The raids continued for the next few years and among the targets were St David's Catholic Cathedral, which was totally destroyed, and Llandaff Cathedral, which was severely damaged. The last air raid on Cardiff was on 18 May 1943, and my research shows that it was a revenge attack for the Dambusters raid on the Ruhr area of Germany the night before. Cardiff was chosen because the Dambusters were led by Guy Gibson, who was married to Eva Turner from Penarth. The then leader of the ARP, Gilbert Shepherd, said: 'The raid was planned by a Nazi who knew his Cardiff.' That Nazi was almost certainly Hans Henri Kühnemann, who was the managing director of the Flottmann Drill Factory in Allansbank Road, between 1935 and 1939. Gilbert Shepherd was also on the board.

Featured in this book is a copy of Kühnemann's Nazi membership card, together with a similar document for Friedrich Schoberth, who was the German lecturer at Cardiff University from 1927 and 1939. When I met Schoberth in Nuremberg in 1986, he told me that during the war he was editor of the propaganda programmes broadcast by Lord Haw-Haw, William Joyce, who lived in Column Road, Cardiff, in the 1930s and was hanged for treason in 1946.

Labour candidates elected to Parliament for Cardiff seats for the first time in 1945 rose to some of the highest positions in the land. James Callaghan, later Lord Callaghan, held the posts of Home Secretary, Chancellor of the Exchequer and Prime Minister. George Thomas was a junior minister at the Home Office, Secretary of State for Wales and Speaker of the House of Commons, a role which resulted in his elevation to the rank of Viscount Tonypandy.

Cardiff Castle.
(*Western Mail and Echo*)

In the late 1940s, Cardiff struggled to recover from the damage inflicted during the war. Men returning from the battlefields and prison camps had difficulty finding work in an era when building restrictions were still in force and where overseas markets were limited. The harsh winter of 1947, when deep snowdrifts brought everything to a standstill, was a testing time for families.

The early 1950s were not much better. Rationing was still in force and jobs were still scarce. In 1952 Mahmood Mattan was the last man to be executed at Cardiff Prison. Forty-six years later he was given a posthumous pardon, following an appeal and a campaign which I started in 1969; it was revived by solicitor Bernard de Maid in the 1990s.

In the 1950s there was a new star shining on the entertainment side. Singer Shirley Bassey, who was born in Bute Street, started along her road to fame by singing in the local Rainbow Club. In 1955, Cardiff was declared the capital of Wales and a new air of confidence was felt. In the swinging '60s, Cardiff started to take off. Building restrictions were long gone and new council estates were springing up on the edge

AN INTRODUCTION

of the city. Leo Abse, then a Labour councillor and later MP for Pontypool and Torfaen, threatened to take a hammer to a wall which was proposed to be built between the private and council houses at Llanrumney.

It was in the 1960s that the Most Revd John Murphy became Roman Catholic Archbishop and Bishop Glyn Simons, of Llandaff, became Anglican Archbishop of Wales. Thousands of Catholic children walked through the crowd-lined streets of the city every year for the traditional Corpus Christi celebrations, which were revived for the first time since the war.

The most significant move made by the city council towards the end of the 1960s was to appoint Professor Colin Buchanan to draw up a blueprint for the capital. Many of his controversial recommendations have helped to reshape the city, but one astounding proposal was defeated He wanted a new road from the north to the south of the city which would have resulted in 30,000 bodies being exhumed from 10,000 graves in Cathays cemetery. The council was ready to give the nod to it, when a by-election in the Conservative stronghold of Penylan was won by Labour's Yvette Roblin, whose one slogan was to 'Stop the Hook Road'.

Llandaff Cathedral. (*Cardiff Central Library*)

More than 150,000 people were at Pontcanna Fields, Cardiff, on 2 June 1982, when Pope John Paul II celebrated a Pontifical High Mass. During lunch at Cardiff Castle he was made a Freeman of Cardiff and in the afternoon he officiated at a service for the young people of Britain at Ninian Park. The following year, the Most Revd John Ward became Roman Catholic Archbishop of Cardiff and joined forces with Anglican and Nonconformist leaders to speak out for the miners who were engaged in a year-long strike. Archbishop Ward resigned in 2001 and was succeeded by Archbishop Peter Smith.

In 1987, the Cardiff Bay Development Corporation was formed and the result of their work can be seen along the growing waterfront. The Bay covers 2,700 acres (1,100 hectares) and its redevelopment was acclaimed as the most important project of its kind in Europe. Among the buildings planned is the home of the National Assembly of Wales, established after a referendum in 1998. A new centre of entertainment will also go there, despite the early failure to build an ultramodern opera house.

The controversial barrage across the bay was completed in 1999, in the hope that it will bring new sporting and social life to the area. The

A CENTURY of CARDIFF

City Hall, Cardiff.
(*Western Mail and Echo*)

designers were confident that it would also end the flooding which had swamped Cardiff on a number of occasions in the twentieth century.

The £120 million Millennium Stadium – it will always be known as the Arms Park to local people – was built by the Welsh Rugby Union with the aid of a grant from the National Lottery fund. It was completed in the autumn of 1999. The former national ground was demolished to make way for it, as was the empire swimming pool. Rugby World Cup matches and the final of the tournament were played at the new stadium in 1999. The trophy was won by Australia.

To mark the Millennium, the BBC staged the biggest *Songs of Praise* event ever, with 66,000 people joining in at the new stadium. It was a fitting amen to twentieth-century Cardiff: an anthem of praise for people from all walks of life who have made the capital of Wales the outstanding city that it is today, a city which was able to host the European Summit in 1998, when leaders of all member countries of the EC met in the Welsh capital. Nelson Mandela, the South African president and a guest of honour, was made a Freeman of Cardiff, an honour he shares with, among others, Winston Churchill and US politician Henry Kissinger. Cardiff is well established on the world stage.

Sadly, as the century drew to a close the City Hall, the jewel in the crown of Cardiff's architecture, was virtually made redundant. It was rejected as the headquarters of the National Assembly for Wales, elected for the first time in May 1999.

The Age of Discovery

Pier Head, Cardiff. (*Arthur Weston Evans Collection*)

A CENTURY of CARDIFF

The laying of the foundation stone for the City Hall, which was completed in 1905. (*South Wales Echo*)

First meeting of council after Cardiff was granted city status in 1905. (*Cardiff Central Library*)

THE AGE OF DISCOVERY

Guests at the Coronation of King Edward VII in 1902: the widowed Marchioness of Bute, her daughter Lady Margaret and sons, the 4th Marquess (right) and Lord Ninian Crichton Stuart, who was elected an MP for Cardiff, and was killed in action in the First World War. (*Cardiff Castle Archives*)

A CENTURY of CARDIFF

Royal yacht arriving at Cardiff on 13 July 1907, to officially open the Queen Alexandra Docks. The Queen and King Edward VII were on board. (*Arthur Weston Evans Collection*)

Crowds line Queen Street during the royal visit in 1907. (*Author's collection*)

THE AGE OF DISCOVERY

Captain Scott (inset) set sail from Cardiff on the *Terra Nova* for his ill-fated exploration of Antarctica in 1910. (*Cardiff Central Library*)

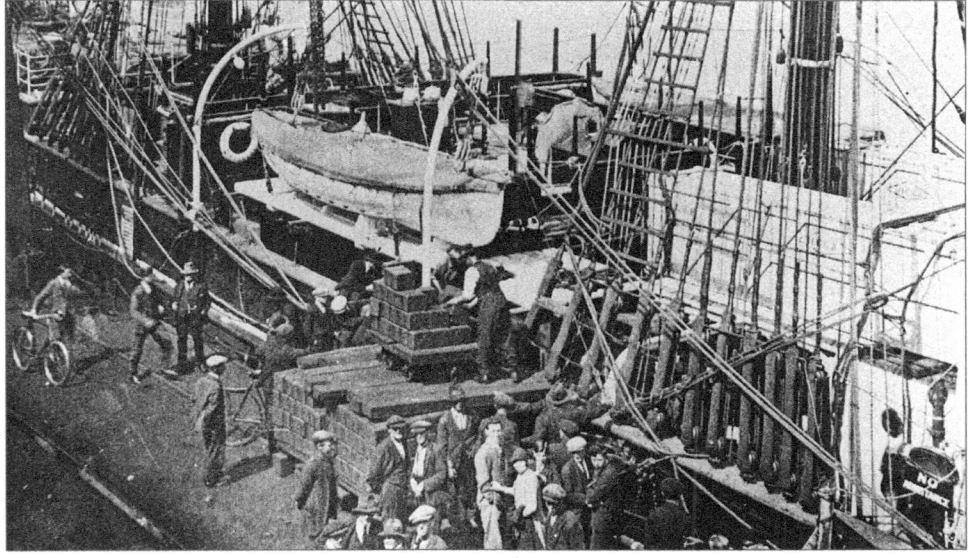

Another of Scott's ships was the *Discovery* which is seen at Cardiff loading fuel donated by the Crown Fuel Company. (*Pope Photographic*)

A CENTURY of CARDIFF

Ernest Willows, who caused a sensation when he launched the first British airship in Cardiff in Edwardian times. Ironically he died in an air balloon accident at Bedford in 1926. (*Alec McKinty's Collection*)

Willows' airship at Pengam Airport. (*Arthur Weston Evans Collection*)

Former *South Wales Echo* Stroller, Alec McKinty, wrote a biography of Willows, entitled *The Father of British Airships*. (*Author's collection*)

THE AGE OF DISCOVERY

The American Roller Rink in Westgate Street, Cardiff. The building was also the hangar where women sewed the panels for barrage balloons, designed by airship pioneer Ernest Willows. (*Author's collection*)

Another air pioneer was Charles Watkins (inset) who, in 1911, was the first pilot to fly over his home city of Cardiff at night. He designed and built the CHW Mono Aircraft which is now on show at the National Museum of Wales. (*Eric Williams Collection*)

A CENTURY of CARDIFF

Young set from Edwardian days outside the Llanishen Post Office, Cardiff. (*Arthur Weston Evans Collection*)

James Street, Cardiff Docks. (*Western Mail and Echo*)

War and Peace

Jim Flynn, of Grangetown, Cardiff, learning to fire a machine gun in the First World War. He was later wounded and was carried three miles to a field hospital by a German soldier. His children include Paul Flynn MP and former Cardiff Councillor Mike Flynn.
(*Mike Flynn*)

Seamen's strike, Cardiff, 1911. Inset, Hancock Wilson (left) and Councillor Chabell. (*Author's collection*)

Opposite, top: The 11th Service Battalion of the Welsh Regiment consisted of 1,000 young men, known as the Cardiff Pals. Some of the Pals are seen on parade at Maindy Stadium. (*Royal Regiment of Wales Museum, Cardiff Castle*)

Opposite, bottom: Still in civilian clothes, the Pals marching down Crwys Road on their way to Cardiff General station where they caught a train to a camp in Sussex. For many of them it was the last time they saw their home city. Hundreds died in action. (*Royal Regiment of Wales Museum, Cardiff Castle*)

WAR AND PEACE

A CENTURY of CARDIFF

Six Cardiff Pals relaxing between the fighting around the Macedonian port of Salonika in 1916. (*Royal Regiment of Wales Museum, Cardiff Castle*)

Suffragettes who volunteered to serve in field hospitals during the
First World War arriving at Cardiff Central station in 1914.
(*Glamorgan Record Office*)

Cardiff-born actor and composer, Ivor Novello, whose song 'Keep the
Home Fires Burning' was a great morale-booster for the men at the front.
(*Ivor Novello Foundation*)

Married at St Margaret's, Roath, on Christmas Day 1918, were George Williams and Lucy Wilkins. (*Eric Williams Collection*)

The young bridesmaid, at the 1918 wedding above, was Lucy Warren who became a well-known teacher in Cardiff and was still active and an ace Scrabble player in the year 2000 at the age of ninety-two. She died in 2001. (*Author's collection*)

Between the Wars

A statue of Peerless Jim Driscoll, Cardiff's legendary boxer, stands in Bute Street, Cardiff. (*Author's collection*)

Boxer Peerless Jim Driscoll was also president of St David's Rugby Team. (*Author's collection*)

The headstone on Peerless Jim's grave wrongly describes him as champion of the world, a title he never won. He gave up the chance of fighting for the crown to return to his home town of Cardiff from America in order to take part in an exhibition bout to raise funds for Nazareth House orphanage. (*Author's collection*)

Opposing captains, Fred Keenor, Cardiff, and Charlie Buchan, Arsenal, shaking hands at the 1927 final of the FA Cup in which Cardiff beat Arsenal 1-0. (*Author's collection*)

Below: Hughie Ferguson, who is not in the picture, put the ball past the Arsenal goalkeeper, Dan Lewis, to bring the FA Cup to Cardiff in 1927. Cardiff's Len Davies is shepherding the ball home. (*Author's collection*)

A CENTURY *of* CARDIFF

BETWEEN THE WARS

A gathering of the Bute Clan at Cardiff Castle in August 1928. The occasion was a garden party to mark the coming of age of the 5th Marquess of Bute, flanked by two ladies in the second row. The 4th Marquess is the one holding his hat in the front row. Next to him is his wife and in the centre is the Dowager Marchioness of Bute. Twenty years after this picture was taken, the 5th Marquess gave the castle to the people of Cardiff. (*Cardiff Castle Archives*)

Up to 10,000 people held an all night vigil, singing hymns and saying the rosary, outside Cardiff prison on 27 January 1928, the day that Danny Driscoll and Edward Rowlands were hanged for the murder of David Lewis in what was known as the 'race gang' killing. As Driscoll walked to the scaffold the crowd sang 'Oh Danny Boy'. Solicitor Bernard de Maid is gathering evidence in an attempt to get a posthumous pardon for Driscoll. (*National Newspaper Library*)

A cabinet radiogram was presented to Father of the Chapel Harry Mees in January 1928, when he celebrated fifty years in the linotype department of the *Western Mail*. (*National Newspaper Library*)

BETWEEN THE WARS

Haulier G.C. Wadsworth's Junior ready to set off from Cardiff in 1931 with a full size doll's house, a gift from the people of Wales for the young Princesses Elizabeth and Margaret Rose. The house, which resembles the main entrance of Llandough Hospital, was made by apprentices who helped build the hospital. The doll's house stands in the royal gardens at Windsor Castle. (*Arthur Weston Evans Collection*)

A sad reflection of Cardiff in the 1930s as remembered by artist Jack Sullivan. This was a typical scene at the junction of James Street and Bute Street, known to the locals as Penniless Point. Out-of-work seamen waited to beg a handout from more fortunate men signing-off from a ship. (*Jack Sullivan*)

Taff swim competitors in Cardiff in the 1930s. When the river became too polluted the annual event took place at Roath Park. Second left in the back row is Gordon Williams, a brilliant young commercial artist who was killed while serving with the RAF in Southern Rhodesia (now Zimbabwe) in 1944. (*Eric Williams Collection*)

When Marion Williams opened a hairdresser's shop in Whitchurch, in 1934, she was quite happy shaving men with an open razor. At the turn of the century Marion's son Terry's hairdressing shop was in Merthyr Road, Whitchurch. (*Family picture*)

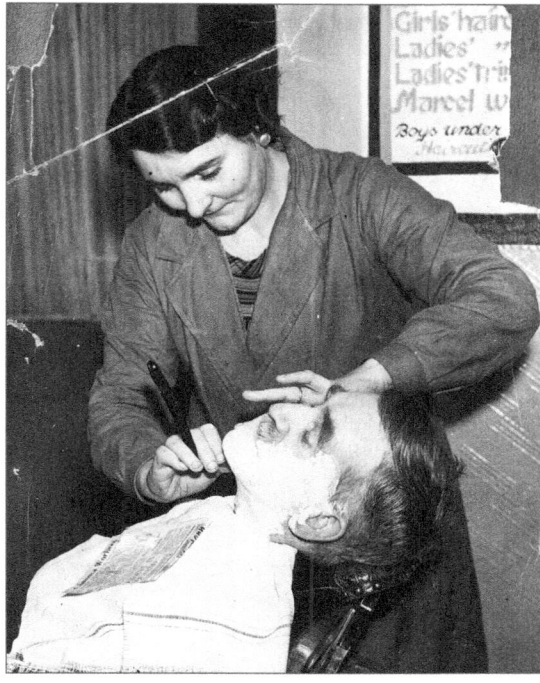

The first hairdressing school was opened in Woodville Road, Cardiff, in 1925. (*Eric Williams Collection*)

A CENTURY of CARDIFF

Workers at the German-owned Flottmann Drill Factory at Allansbank Road, Cardiff. Their boss from 1935 to 1939 was Hans Henri Kühnemann, Hitler's top spy in Wales. (*Author's collection*)

Below: A copy of Kühnemann's Nazi membership card which shows his links with Cardiff and Newport. He almost certainly helped to plan the last air raid on Cardiff, on 18 May 1943. It was said to be in revenge for the Dambusters' raid on Germany the night before, a raid led by Wing Commander Guy Gibson who was married to actress Eva Turner, from Penarth. (*Author's collection*)

Under Attack

American troops disembarking at Cardiff in 1943.
(*Arthur Weston Evans Collection*)

A CENTURY of CARDIFF

CITY OF CARDIFF
AIR RAID (GENERAL) PRECAUTIONS SCHEME

The City Council Invite the ENROLMENT of VOLUNTEERS of both sexes for service in an emergency in connection with the Air Raid (General) Precautions Scheme.

The Volunteers are required for the following purposes, viz.:—

(a) First-aid Parties;
(b) First-aid Posts;
(c) Ambulance Services;
(d) Rescue, Demolition and Clearance of Debris Squads;
(e) Decontamination Squads;
(f) Report Centre Staffs;
(g) Messengers;
(h) Clerks, Storekeepers, &c.

Persons who are willing to offer the service of vehicles, such as private cars, motor-vans, or lorries, for the conveyance of wounded and of men and materials in time of emergency, are requested to register their vehicles for these purposes.

All Volunteers will be given general air raid precautions training and specialised training for their particular service.

Men under 30 years of age, reservists of any branch of the Fighting Services and members of the Territorial Army or Auxiliary Air Force, are not eligible for enrolment.

Forms of enrolment and registration, together with further particulars, can be obtained at the Air Raid Precautions Bureau, City Hall, Cardiff, which will be open between the hours of 9.0 a.m. and 8.0 p.m. on weekdays, excluding Saturdays, and 9.0 a.m. and 1.0 p.m. on Saturdays.

City Hall, Cardiff.
22nd April, 1938.

D. KENVYN REES,
Town Clerk.

Preparing for war. (*Author's collection*)

The cartoonist on the *South Wales Echo*, J.C. Walker, captured the mood of the country on Armistice Day, 11 November 1939, the 21st anniversary of the end of the First World War. (*National Newspaper Library*)

UNDER ATTACK

Nurses leaving the Cardiff Royal Infirmary after it had been hit by bombs in 1941.
(*Imperial War Museum*)

Albany Road after an air raid in 1941.
(*Western Mail and Echo*)

A CENTURY of CARDIFF

St David's Roman Catholic Cathedral, Charles Street, was destroyed by incendiary bombs in a raid on 4 March 1941. It was not rebuilt until 1959. (*Imperial War Museum*)

Canon Patrick Creed, who risked his life to carry the Blessed Sacrament from the burning cathedral which was bombed while he was firewatching. He died in February 2000 after serving for forty-three years as parish priest of St Teilo's, Whitchurch. (*Author*)

Women making tank parts at the ROF factory in Llanishen. (*Author's collection*)

Archbishop Michael McGrath conducting a graveside service for some of the people who were killed in an air raid in 1941. (*Western Mail and Echo*)

Wartime Prime Minister Winston Churchill was mobbed when he visited Cardiff after the blitz in 1941. (*Imperial War Museum*)

The Riverside Conservative Club was destroyed in the blitz of 1 and 2 January 1941. The club had been opened by Churchill in 1922 and he promised to look after the plaque he unveiled until the club was rebuilt. A spokesman at the club said he didn't know what had happened to the plaque. (*Imperial War Museum*)

Churchill visits Cardiff Royal Infirmary, 1941. (*Western Mail and Echo*)

A CENTURY *of* CARDIFF

UNDER ATTACK

American troops based at
Maindy Barracks before
D-Day, 6 June 1944.
(*Royal Regiment of Wales
Museum, Cardiff Castle*)

The Cardiff firm of Davies, Middleton and Davies was involved in making a special roll-up tank track which was used in the D-Day invasion. Secret trials were carried out at Cardiff Docks.
(*Imperial War Museum*)

Cardiff's most notorious resident was Irishman William Joyce, who was known as Lord Haw-Haw when he broadcast German propaganda to Britain during the Second World War. In the 1930s Joyce lived in Column Road, Cardiff. In 1946 he was hanged for treason. (*Imperial War Museum*)

A copy of the Nazi card of Dr Friedrich Schoberth, who was head of German at the University of Wales, Cardiff, between 1927 and 1939. He told the author at Nuremburg in 1986 that he was Lord Haw-Haw's editor during the Second World War. (*Author's collection*)

Dr Schoberth also told the author that he did not help to plan air raids on Cardiff. 'How could I? My daughter is buried at Llanishen Churchyard.' Helga Elizabeth Schoberth was four when she died of meningitis in 1937. (*Author*)

Cardiff's Deputy Mayor, Councillor Chris Bettison, a lecturer at the university, is seen putting flowers on the child's grave. (*Author*)

A CENTURY of CARDIFF

Above: Taffy, the regimental goat, bows gracefully to Princess Elizabeth, the future Queen, when she visited Cardiff in 1948. (*Royal Regiment of Wales Museum, Cardiff Castle*)

Queen Elizabeth admiring the regimental goat during a visit to Cardiff in the late 1940s. (*Royal Regiment of Wales Museum, Cardiff Castle*)

UNDER ATTACK

Jim Callaghan was first elected as MP for Cardiff South-East in 1945. He is seen making a point to local dockers in 1948. (*Western Mail and Echo*)

Below: The Glamorgan Corps of the ATS on parade at Maindy Barracks, Cardiff, on St David's Day, 1948. (*Royal Regiment of Wales Museum, Cardiff Castle*)

A CENTURY of CARDIFF

Members of the 77th Ack Ack, who spent years in Japanese prisoner-of-war camps, were welcomed home by Alderman W.R. Wills, Lord Mayor of Cardiff. (*Western Mail and Echo*)

When the Welsh College of Music and Drama opened in 1948, one of its first students was actor and comedian Victor Spinetti (left). He is seen more than forty years later with Dr George Guest, leader of St John's Choir at Cambridge; actor Kenneth Griffiths and Sir Geraint Evans. (*College Archives*)

Welcome to Empire

Boxer Malcolm Collins, flag-bearer at the 1958 Commonwealth Games.
(*Malcolm Collins Collection*)

A CENTURY of CARDIFF

The Welsh Rugby XV which won the Triple Crown in 1952. (*Author's collection*)

National Service recruits are introduced to weapon training at Maindy Barracks in 1952. (*Royal Regiment of Wales Museum, Cardiff Castle*)

WELCOME TO EMPIRE

Art students in Cardiff in the mid-1950s. (*Eric Williams Collection*)

The 50-metre swimming pool which was built for the Empire Games in 1958. It was demolished in the late 1990s when the Millennium Stadium was built nearby. (*Author*)

A CENTURY of CARDIFF

WELCOME TO EMPIRE

Runner Ron Jones hands the traditional message to the Duke of Edinburgh at the start of the Empire Games in Cardiff in 1958. (*Western Mail and Echo*)

Malcolm Collins fighting gold medal winner W. Taylor, of Australia, in the Featherweight final at the Empire Games in Cardiff, 1958. Taylor was down for a count of nine in the third round but still won on points. (*Malcolm Collins Collection*)

Below: Closing ceremony at the Empire Games in 1958. (*Malcolm Collins Collection*)

The Memorable '60s

Shirley Bassey in 1964. (*Author's collection*)

A CENTURY of CARDIFF

Shirley Bassey at the Rainbow Club, Cardiff, early 1960s. (*Author's collection*)

Shirley Bassey is still a great favourite after forty years. She brought the house down when she wore this Welsh flag dress at the World Rugby Cup finals in Cardiff and at Millennium concerts. (*Wales News*)

THE MEMORABLE '60s

Fr Sean Kearney with altar boys at St David's Cathedral in the 1950s. Do you recognise the boy second from left in the second row? It's the future Welsh Rugby scrum-half Terry Holmes. (*Collection of John Adams*, who is on the far right of the picture)

Former altar boy Terry Holmes in action for Cardiff at the Arms Park. (*Western Mail and Echo*)

Another poser. Who's the Cross Bearer? It's folk singer David Burns with altar boys in David Street, Cardiff, in the 1960s. His brother Michael is the acolyte on the right. (*John Adams Collection*)

The Hennessys, David Burns (right), Frank Hennessy (centre) and Iolo Jones. (*David Burns Collection*)

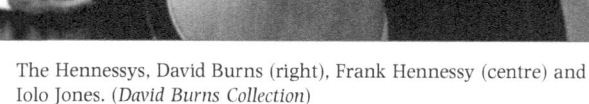

Outstanding folk singer Heather Jones who often shares gigs with The Hennessys. (*David Burns Collection*)

THE MEMORABLE '60s

Leading Muslims heading for the City Hall to examine plans for Bute Town. (*Western Mail and Echo*)

A scene at the entrance to Cardiff Docks as remembered by artist Jack Sullivan. He is the docks policeman on the right. The police constable depicted on the left was Viv Brooks who rose to become Assistant Chief Constable of South Wales.

A CENTURY *of* CARDIFF

Miners on parade in Cardiff in the 1960s. (*Western Mail and Echo*)

Below: Sister Teresita with pupils of St Joseph's Convent School, in Corpus Christi procession, 1964. (*Author's collection*)

THE MEMORABLE '60s

Above: Mother Teresa (centre) arriving at Cardiff General station in 1969. (*Author's collection*)

In 1966, the women of Newtown, Cardiff's Little Ireland, held a wake to mark the end of their estate. It was demolished 120 years after it had been built in a hurry to house Irish refugees from the great famine of 1845 to 1849. (*Mary Sullivan's collection*)

THE MEMORABLE '60s

A strike at the Cardiff Dry Docks in January, 1967, made the national headlines. The author covered the story for the *Daily Mail* for which he was then working. (*Dennis Stephens*)

A CENTURY of CARDIFF

Relaxing at an occasion at St Illtyd's College (left to right): Brother Alexander, Archbishop John Murphy, Sir Charles Hallinan, George Thomas MP, Jim Callaghan MP, Brother Victor and Bishop Mullins. (*Author*)

Twisting the night away at a dance in Cardiff in the 1960s. (*D.I. Jenkins*)

THE MEMORABLE '60s

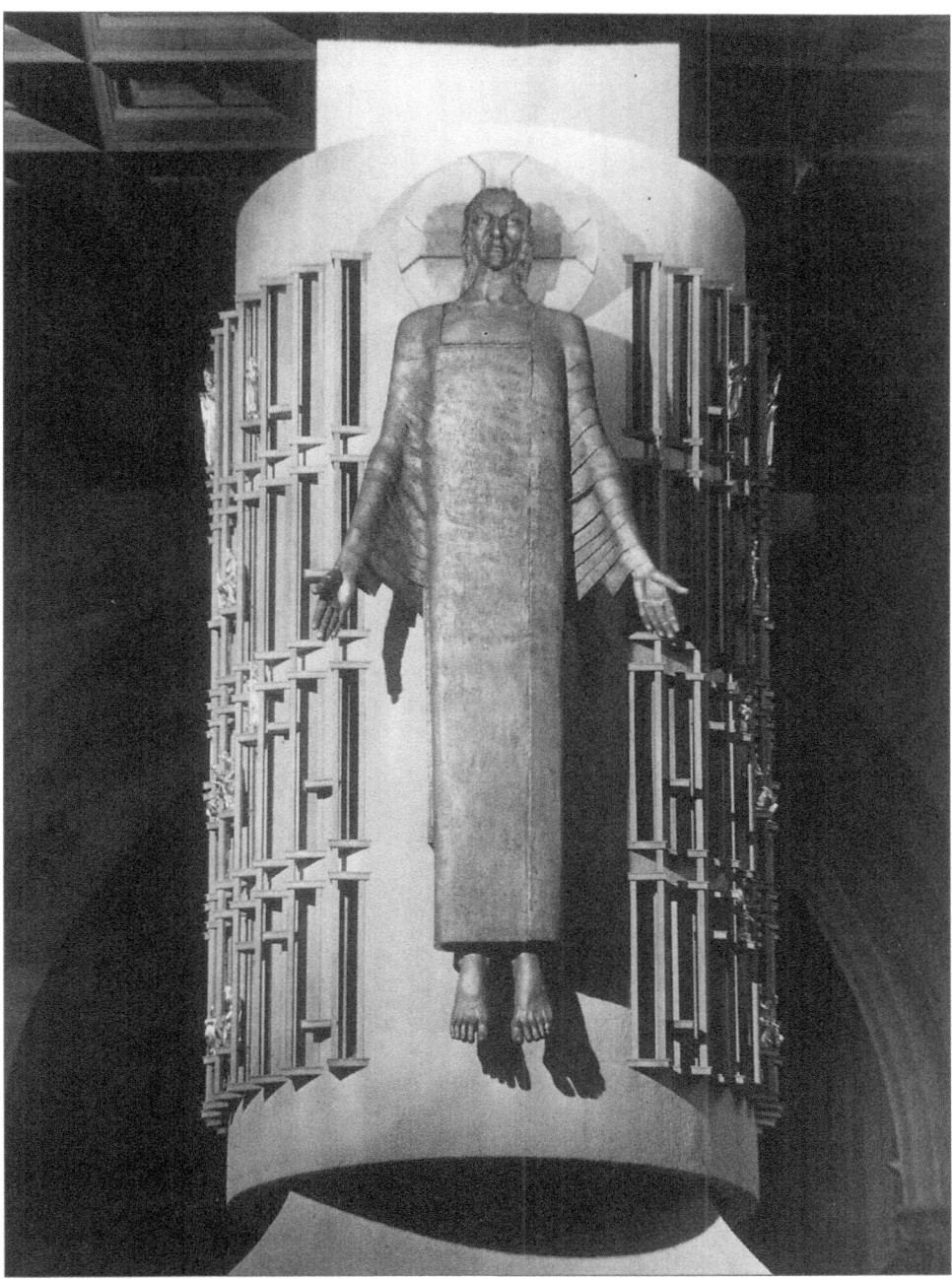

Epstein's statue of the Risen Christ which caused a sensation when it was unveiled at Llandaff Cathedral. (*Cardiff Central Library*)

A CENTURY of CARDIFF

Cardiff Rugby Club annual reunion, 1961. Left to right, Hubert Johnson, Bobby Dalahay, R.T. Gabe, H.M. Chapman, Commander D.J. Tarr, C.R.G. Harris and G. Chapman. (*Western Mail and Echo*)

Leo Abse, MP, a Cardiff solicitor who stole the show on budget days with his flamboyant outfits. (*Western Mail and Echo*)

Dannie Abse, Leo's brother, who won fame as a poet. (*Western Mail and Echo*)

76

The Road to Fame

If ever television personality and broadcaster Sue Lawley runs short of ideas for her *Desert Island Discs* programme she could turn to former colleagues at the *South Wales Echo* and *Western Mail*, where she trained as a journalist in the 1960s. (*BBC*)

Best selling author Ken Follett, another *Echo* trainee. (*Ken's agent*)

Alun Michael MP left the *South Wales Echo* to work with young people. He served as a city councillor before being elected as a Labour Member of Parliament. He was appointed Secretary of State for Wales and after a few short months became the First Secretary of the National Assembly for Wales. He resigned the post early in 2000 after a major controversy over Euro funds. (*Western Mail and Echo*)

Mike Buerk, a *South Wales Echo* reporter in the 1960s, shook the conscience of the world when he reported for the BBC on the Ethiopian famine of the 1980s. He returned from Africa to front BBC television news programmes. (*BBC*)

THE ROAD TO FAME

Former *Western Mail* reporter, Cardiff-born John Humphrys, is one of the BBC's top journalists and interviewers. Through the Radio Four *Today* programme his voice is known to millions. (*Author's collection*)

John's brother, Bob Humphrys, who left the *Western Mail*, where he specialised in feature writing, in 1978. He joined BBC Wales and became an award-winning sports editor. (*BBC Wales*)

Geraint Stanley Davies, a *Western Mail* journalist who rose to become Controller of BBC Wales. (*BBC Wales*)

Donald Woods, who worked on the *Western Mail* sub-editor's table, wrote the biography of South African anti-apartheid martyr Steve Biko, used as the basis of the blockbuster film *Cry Freedom*, which awakened the conscience of the world to the evils of apartheid. (*Western Mail and Echo*)

Former *Echo* leader writer James Tucker, who writes crime novels as Bill James, David Craig, and Judith Jones. A Bill James novel called *Protection* was adapted and shown on BBC TV in 1996. (*Western Mail and Echo*)

From writing features for the *Echo* Herbert Williams graduated to radio and television. A poet and short-story writer, Herbert has also written some valuable non-fiction books. These include *Come Out Wherever You Are*, the story of the great escape by German prisoners of war from Island Farm Camp at Bridgend in the 1940s. His television scripts include the *Life and Death of Dylan Thomas* for BBC2. (*Author's collection*)

THE ROAD TO FAME

What's a Bishop doing among journalists? Richard Williamson was a reporter with the *Echo* from 1961 to 1962 and with the *Western Mail* from 1962 to 1963. In 1976, Richard was ordained a dinosaur-Catholic priest by the Archbishop Lefebvre; in 1988, he was consecrated a dinosaur-Catholic bishop by Lefebvre, the French church leader who broke away from the Vatican. Richard sent this photograph from the Seminary of the dinosaur-Catholic Society of St Pius X, in Minnesota, USA, where he is Rector.

John Greally returned to the *Western Mail* as a journalist after trying his vocation as a Jesuit priest. He has written a novel and composed symphonies and hymns. (*Western Mail and Echo*)

The Revd Roy Jenkins who left the *South Wales Echo* to become a Baptist minister and later became head of religious broadcasting at BBC Wales. (*BBC Wales*)

A CENTURY of CARDIFF

Controversial columnist Dan O'Neill tastes a new brew from Cardiff's long established brewery, S.A. Brain. (*Western Mail and Echo*)

Dan as a toddler. What's the betting that he had half-a-dark in his bottle? (*Mike Flynn's Collection*)

Lionel Fanthorpe was a headteacher in the 1960s but got on his bike, was ordained a priest by the Church in Wales and, as the Reverend Rev-up, rode around on his Harley Davidson. He became famous as a broadcaster, television personality, author, ghost-buster and *Echo* columnist. (*Author's collection*)

Jim's Den – No. 10

Cardiff South-East MP James Callaghan who held office as Foreign
Secretary, Chancellor of the Exchequer and Prime Minister, in the 1970s.
(*Western Mail and Echo*)

A CENTURY of CARDIFF

US Secretary of State, Henry Kissinger, was given the Freedom of Cardiff in 1975. He is flanked by the then Chancellor of the Exchequer, Jim Callaghan, and Secretary of State for Wales, George Thomas. (*Western Mail and Echo*)

Prime Minister, Jim Callaghan, shakes hands with his Cardiff driver John Heggarty at the opening of the Maritime and Industrial Museum in April 1977. (*Western Mail and Echo*)

George Thomas, MP for Cardiff West, became Speaker of the House of Commons in 1979. When he retired he became Viscount Tonypandy. (*Author's collection*)

Sir Julian Hodge, philanthropist and founder of the Bank of Wales, at Buckingham Palace after being knighted in 1970. With him are Lady Hodge, and their children, Julian, Jane and Robert. Sir Julian died on Jersey at the age of 99 in 2004. (*Author's collection*)

A CENTURY of CARDIFF

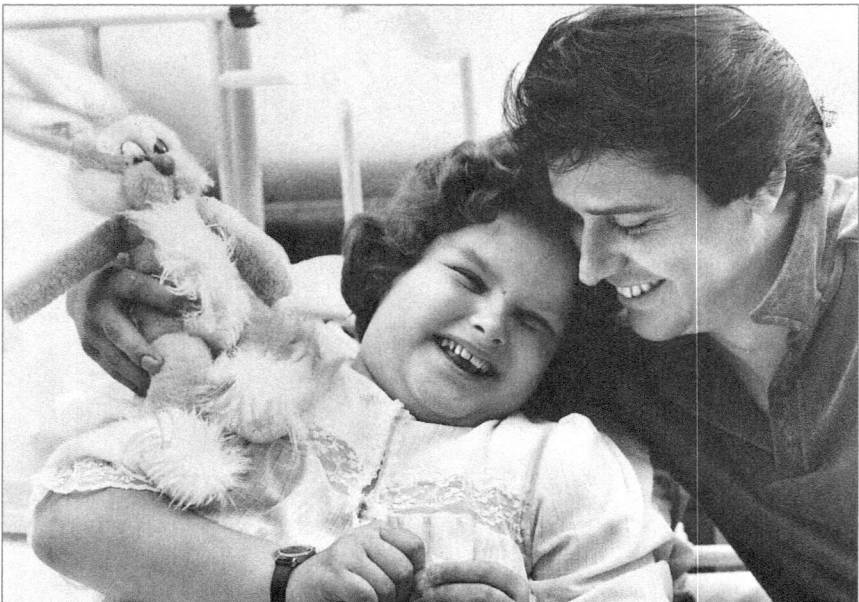

Above: Members of the Cardiff branch of the National Union of Journalists joined the fight to save mining and steel jobs in Wales in the 1970s. (*Terry Downey*)

Cardiff-born chart topper Shakin' Stevens whose music helped to save the life of Wendy Downham, who had been in a coma for eleven days. (*Western Mail and Echo*)

The 1980s and a Papal Visit

Echo seller on the day of the papal visit, 1982.

Pope John Paul II driving through Cardiff in the car nicknamed The Popemobile. (*Western Mail and Echo*)

The banner says it all at a youth service at Ninian Park, Cardiff. (*Western Mail and Echo*)

THE 1980s AND A PAPAL VISIT

The Pope celebrates holy communion at the papal mass, Pontcanna Fields, Cardiff. (*Western Mail and Echo*)

Crowd outside Cardiff Castle hoping to catch a glimpse of the Pope on 2 June 1982. (*Universe*)

THE 1980s AND A PAPAL VISIT

Trying to get a better view! (*Universe*)

In December 1980, the Revd Iris Thomas was the first woman in the Llandaff diocese to be ordained an Anglican deacon. More than a dozen members of the congregation walked out of Llandaff Cathedral in protest at the move. It took the Church in Wales another fifteen years to allow women to be ordained as priests and Iris was one of the first in line. (*Author*)

Below: Edward Davies (left) was ordained a priest and his wife Sally a deacon in a joint ceremony at Llandaff Cathedral, in 1991. They are seen talking to the Rt Revd Roy Davies, Bishop of Llandaff, who performed the ceremonies. In 1997, Sally was ordained a priest. (*Western Mail and Echo*)

THE 1980s AND A PAPAL VISIT

Cardiff Internationals, known as the CIACS, have produced many fine rugby players. Here is some of the team with the array of trophies they won in 1986. (*Western Mail and Echo*)

Ace walker Steve Barry (No. 3) taking part in a race with members of Roath Labour Club. He won the six mile event in a record time of 42 mins 52 secs. He is cheered on by his father Dai Barry (left), who was the proudest man in Wales when Steve struck gold in the 30km walk at the Commonwealth Games in Brisbane, Australia, in 1982.
(*Western Mail and Echo*)

Guide dog owner Ken Williams had the shock of his life when he was told that his gold labrador Abel was also blind and had been for a number of years. Abel had to retire but Ken kept him as a pet after being provided with a black labrador, Gay. The Guide Dogs for the Blind Association has opened a training school in Cardiff. (*Author*)

The 1990s

Security was tight for the European Summit and the visit of Nelson Mandela in 1998. The crew of the security balloon, seen passing Cardiff Castle, had a bird's eye view of the city.
(*Western Mail and Echo*)

A CENTURY of CARDIFF

Former South African President Nelson Mandela with children at Cardiff Castle when he received the Freedom of the City on 16 June 1998. (*County Hall Collection*)

Nelson Mandela makes friends with the choir at Cardiff Castle. (*County Hall Collection*)

THE 1990s

A smiling Mandela greets the crowds in Park Place, Cardiff. (*Western Mail and Echo*)

Head teacher Betty Campbell with some of her pupils at Mount Stuart School, Cardiff Bay. (*Western Mail and Echo*)

A CENTURY of CARDIFF

Prime Minister Tony Blair greets the Dutch delegation which attended the European Summit in Cardiff in June 1998. (*Western Mail and Echo*)

Neil and Glenys Kinnock, both graduates of University College of Wales, Cardiff. Neil became leader of the Labour Party and a European Commissioner. Glenys was elected as a member of the European Parliament.

Rhodri and Julie Morgan, husband and wife, who were both elected to represent Cardiff constituencies in the House of Commons. Rhodri succeeded Alun Michael as First Secretary of the National Assembly for Wales which was established in 1999.

THE 1990s

Diana, Princess of Wales, joins in the singing of the Welsh national anthem at the National Ground in Cardiff. (*Western Mail and Echo*)

Prince Charles chatting to singer Iris Williams at the opening of the extension to the Welsh College of Music and Drama. In the background is opera star Dame Gwyneth Jones. (*Brian Tarr*)

A CENTURY of CARDIFF

Welsh children dancing for Crown Princess Martha Louise Marie of Norway at the opening of the relocated Norwegian church at The Bay in 1995. (*Norwegian church*)

The Norwegian church, now an arts and culture centre, a prominent landmark at Cardiff Bay. (*Norwegian church*)

Bishop Roy Davies, of Llandaff, conducting a service at the Lightship, which has been converted into a church at Cardiff Bay. (*Author*)

THE 1990s

The Millennium Stadium, built with the help of a National Lottery Grant at a cost of £120 million. It was completed in time to host the Rugby World Cup, won by Australia in the autumn of 1999. Following the demolition of Wembley, the Millennium Stadium was chosen to host the FA Cup Final in the year 2001.

Pupils of St Cuthbert's, Bute Town, with artist Jack Sullivan in front of the Merchant Navy memorial they helped to create. It is believed to be the only memorial in Britain to feature a black man. Jack toured city schools in the 1990s talking about his life and encouraging young artists. He had more than 2,000 thank-you letters from children. (*Western Mail and Echo*)

One of the great characters of Cardiff in the 1990s was man of the road Charlie Parsons who wheeled his worldly belongings around in a shopping trolley as he took his many four-legged friends for a walk. Artist Jack Sullivan features him talking to John Thomson of Bute Town. (*Jack Sullivan*)

The Pakistani Ambassador (left) at a function in the city where he did part of his training as a journalist on the Thomson Foundation Course. (*Author*)

Nicky Delgado visited many parts of the world before returning to his native city of Cardiff where he reads the poetry he writes. (*Author's collection*)

Cardiff has a reputation as a centre for kidney transplants and one of the most moving stories concerned Lyn and Helen King. Lyn sacrificed one of his kidneys in the spring of 1999 to enable his wife to have a transplant operation, which was a success. Sadly, weeks later Helen died suddenly of a mysterious virus at the University Hospital of Wales. (*Western Mail and Echo*)

When fanatical animal lover Helen died, donations in her memory were sent to the Kidney Research Unit Foundation for Wales. Another animal lover, Betty French (pictured here), of Pentyrch, Cardiff, raised more than £1,000 by completing a sponsored 80-mile ride from Carmarthen to Cardiff to celebrate her seventy-ninth birthday in June 1999. (*Author's collection*)

THE 1990s

Cathays cemetery at the unveiling, on St Patrick's Day 1999, of the memorial to victims of the great Irish famine (1845–9) and all Irish people who have lived and died in Wales. Speaking is Tyrone O'Sullivan, who was hailed as the man who saved Tower Colliery, Hirwaun, the last deep pit in South Wales from closing. (*Author*)

Guests at the unveiling of the memorial included the Lord Lieutenant, Captain Norman Lloyd Edwards, the Consular General for Ireland in Wales, Conor O'Reirdon, Welsh Office Minister John Owen Jones and the Lord Mayor of Cardiff, Marion Drake. (*Author*)

A CENTURY of CARDIFF

The fight against famine in the world continues. Chris Williams, of Christian Aid, is seen outside the City Hall collecting signatures for the Jubilee 2000 petition to persuade rich countries to reduce third world debts. (*Author*)

The Princess Royal came to Cardiff to open the new Mission to Seamen's headquarters. She is seen chatting to the chairman of the Mission, Bob Chatterton, and artist Jack Sullivan who presented her with one of his paintings. (*Jack Sullivan*)

THE 1990s

The cruiser HMS *Cardiff* on the high seas. (*Ministry of Defence*)

A CENTURY of CARDIFF

The previous HMS *Cardiff* which led the surrendered German fleet into Scapa Flow in 1918. The Germans later scuttled their vessels. (*Imperial War Museum*)

Echo cartoonist Gren's view of HMS *Kairdiff* – that's how the Kairdiff Language Society spells the name of the city! (*Gren's collection*)

"The ship's painter is from somewhere called Grangetown."

Echo cartoonist Gren, creator of a million smiles. (*Author's collection*)

THE 1990s

HTV television personalities and executives celebrating the award of a new franchise. (*HTV Archives*)

A CENTURY of CARDIFF

Cardiff-born Jeremy Bowen reported for BBC television from many war zones, including Kosovo, where this photograph was taken. (*BBC*)

The contribution of broadcaster and playwright Saunders Lewis to the Welsh language and cultural life in Wales is immeasurable. Saunders was a founder of the Welsh Nationalist Party and died in 1985. (*Author's collection*)

Old Illtydian Vincent Kane has been an outstanding broadcaster for BBC Wales radio and television for more than three decades. (*BBC*)

THE 1990s

Silence of the Lambs Oscar winner, Sir Anthony Hopkins, is a graduate of the Welsh College of Music and Drama in Cardiff. (*College Archives*)

Singer Iris Williams, who was a student at the Welsh College of Music and Drama in the 1960s, made it big in America and many other parts of the world. She often recalled the days when she was living at the Sisters of Charity hostel for students in Cathedral Road, Cardiff. (*Author's collection*)

The Cardiff schoolgirl with the golden voice, Charlotte Church, talking to the Duchess of Kent. (*Western Mail and Echo*)

The Cardiff-based chart-topping group Catatonia. (*Agent*)

A CENTURY of CARDIFF

Two-ton Tessie O'Shea, the Cardiff-born comedy singer whose personality wooed audiences in America and Britain. (*Western Mail and Echo*)

A scene from *Bombs and Bloomers*, staged by the Cardiff-based Hijinx Theatre Company. (*Hijinx Archives*)

Max Boyce, whose songs have made a bigger impact on rugby grounds in Cardiff than Adidas boots. He has been made an Honorary Fellow of the Welsh College of Music and Drama. (*Agent*)

THE 1990s

Cardiff's world boxing champion Steve Robinson. (*Western Mail and Echo*)

Brian Jones who, like Steve Robinson, came from Ely and also won a world title. (*Western Mail and Echo*)

115

Cardiff-born John Toshack's name is known and respected throughout the world of soccer. For a short while he was manager of Wales. (*Western Mail and Echo*)

Another Cardiff man to manage Wales, after an outstanding career as a player, was Terry Yorath. (*Western Mail and Echo*)

Manchester United and Wales striker Ryan Giggs signing autographs in his native city of Cardiff. (*Western Mail and Echo*)

THE 1990s

The Millennium Stadium with its retractable roof in place. (*Wales News*)

Three men whose names are legendary in Welsh rugby, Gareth Edwards, Barry John and Gerald Davies.
(*Western Mail and Echo*)

Welsh international Neil Jenkins, who has scored more points in international rugby than anyone else in the world. He was transferred from Pontypridd to Cardiff in 1999. (*Western Mail and Echo*)

THE 1990s

World champion hurdler, Cardiff's Colin Jackson, in action. (*Western Mail and Echo*)

Paralympic gold medallist and London Marathon winner Tanni Grey-Thompson, one of the outstanding wheelchair athletes in the world. (*Western Mail and Echo*)

Maurice Turnbull, an international rugby, cricket, hockey and squash player, was killed by a sniper's bullet in Normandy on 5 August 1944. (*Western Mail and Echo*)

Wilf Wooller, who captained Glamorgan, was a great all-round sportsman. (*Western Mail and Echo*)

Acknowledgements

I wish to thank the following who made this book possible: the *Western Mail and Echo* and the generations of photographers who worked for the newspapers; the *Universe*; BBC; BBC Wales; HTV; Cardiff Castle archivist, Matthew Williams; Cardiff Central Library; Wales News; National Newspaper Library; Royal Regiment of Wales Museum, Cardiff Castle; Glamorgan Record Office; Cardiff City and County Council; Welsh College of Music and Drama; Cardiff Maritime Museum; Imperial War Museum; artist Jack Sullivan; Eric Williams; Arthur Weston Evans; Mike Flynn; Hilary David, Ivor Novello Foundation; John Adams; David Burns; Mary Sullivan; Brian Tarr; Norwegian Church; Marion Qua.

Plans for the National Assembly of Wales building, designed by Richard Rogers Partnership. The decision to create a new building was taken amid great controversy, as many people wanted the assembly to be housed at the City Hall.